Macmillan/McGraw-Hil
Energy and You

NOISY NICO

AUTHORS

Mary Atwater
The University of Georgia
Prentice Baptiste
University of Houston
Lucy Daniel
Rutherford County Schools
Jay Hackett
University of Northern Colorado
Richard Moyer
University of Michigan, Dearborn
Carol Takemoto
Los Angeles Unified School District
Nancy Wilson
Sacramento Unified School District

Macmillan/McGraw-Hill School Publishing Company
New York Columbus

Noisy Nico

Themes:
Energy / Systems and Interactions

Lessons

Activities!

EXPLORE

TRY THIS

CAREERS

SCIENCE TECHNOLOGY AND Society

Theme T ENERGY

What Is Sound?

Elena's little brother, Nicholás, likes making sound. Elena calls him "Noisy Nico."

People Use Sound

By listening to sounds, people can tell what is happening around them. Just by listening, Elena knows some things that are happening outside her home. What do you think Elena hears? What do you hear where you live?

People also use sound to communicate.

Sometimes they talk.

Sometimes they sing.

Sometimes they laugh.

Minds On! How do you think people make sound? Hold your fingers against your throat. Try growling softly. What do you feel?

EXPLORE

Activity!

What Makes Sound?

What do you think makes sound? Are all sounds made the same way? See if you can find out how sound is made.

What You Need

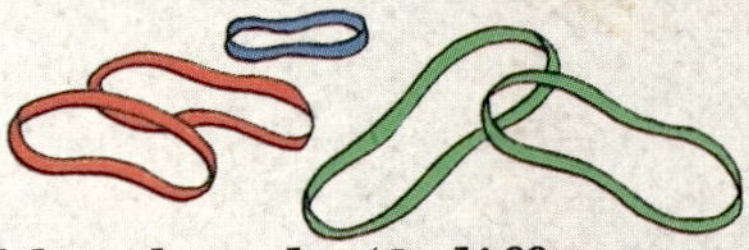

rubber bands (3 different sizes)

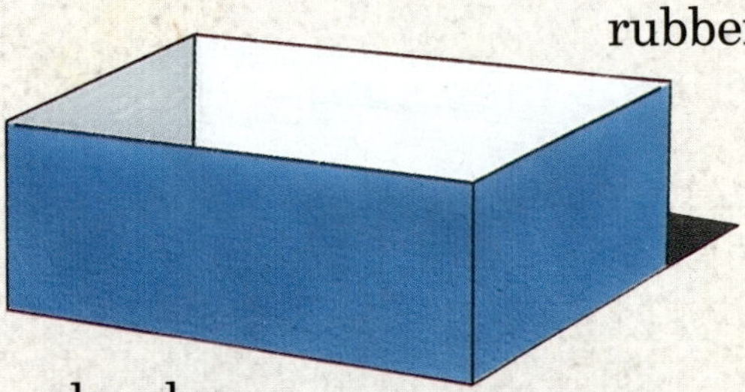

shoe box

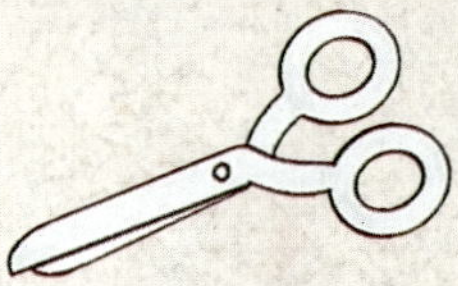

scissors

Activity Log

What To Do

1. Carefully cut 3 slits in each end of the shoe box.

2. Stretch the rubber bands around the box so that they fit in the slits.

Safety! Be careful with scissors and rubber bands!

3. Pluck each rubber band.
   What do you hear?
   What do you feel?
   What do you see?

4. Draw a picture in your ***Activity Log*** of what the rubber bands look like when they are making a sound.

What Happened?

1. What did you observe happen to the rubber bands? What did you hear?
2. How could you make the sounds you hear different? Try it.

Sound Off!

Elena had to get away from Noisy Nico! She went next door to listen to her cousin play her guitar. Elena's cousin has a Spanish guitar.

This guitar has six strings. When the strings are plucked or strummed, they **vibrate.** That means they move back and forth quickly. When guitar strings vibrate, they make sound.

Minds On! What other instruments make sound when you strum or pluck on strings?

Sound is a form of energy. Something must move to make sound. We call these movements **vibrations.** Some things vibrate so quickly you cannot see them move.

Bumblebees move their wings rapidly to make a buzzing sound.

Male crickets rub their wings together to make a chirping sound.

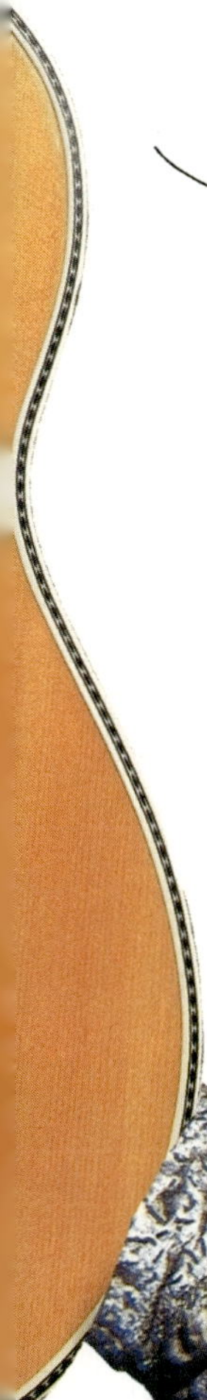

Frogs vibrate their throats to make a croaking sound.

Nico has found another way to make noise!

How do you make a sound with a drum? What part of the drum vibrates? Make a drum in the next activity to find out.

TRY THIS

Activity!

Make Your Own Drum!

What You Need

small coffee can
big, round balloon
scissors
thick rubber band
pencil with eraser
Activity Log

What To Do

1. Cut off the end of the balloon with your scissors.
2. Carefully stretch the balloon over the open end of the coffee can. Hold the balloon in place with the rubber band.
3. Use the eraser end of the pencil as a drumstick and tap your drum. Observe what happens.
4. Write about what you see in your ***Activity Log.***

India

AROUND THE WORLD

Drums have been used for many years by many people all over the world. Look at these drums. How do you think they are used? How do you think they sound?

West Indies

Africa

Canada

People use drums to make music. People have used them to send messages. Some messages told about meetings, but others warned of danger. How would you use a drum to send a message to a friend? How far away could your friend be and still hear your message?

Morocco

Here comes Noisy Nico again!
He has a horn.
What a racket!

When you blow into a horn, you make the air inside vibrate.
To make the air in a horn vibrate,

you blow across a hole in the mouthpiece,

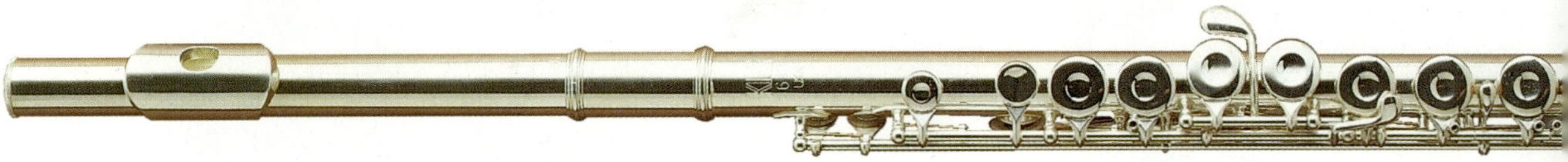

Flute

or you blow and make a reed on the mouthpiece vibrate,

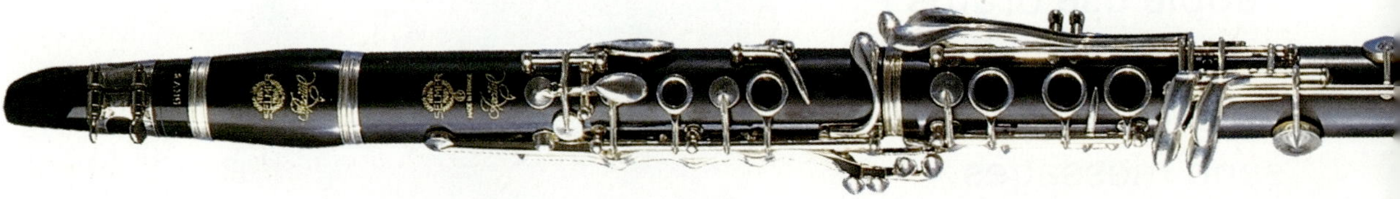

Clarinet

or you make your lips vibrate.

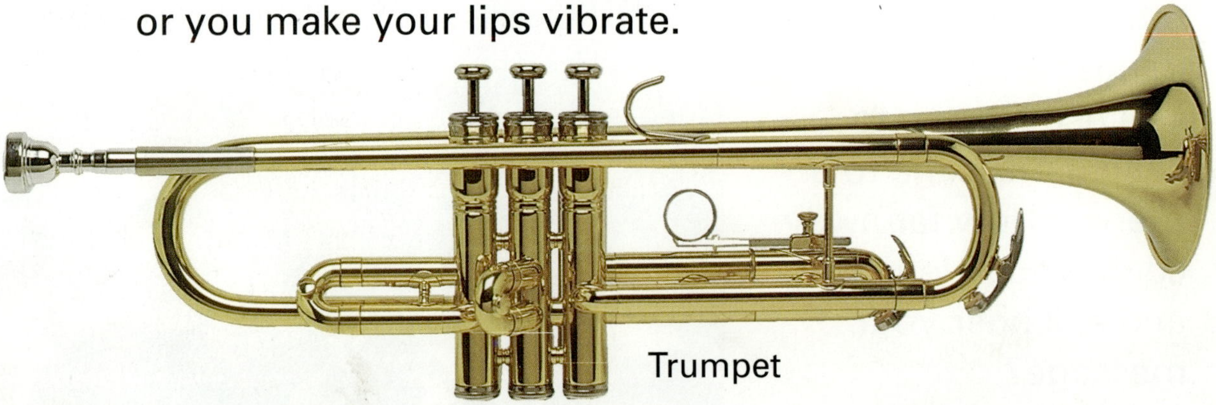

Trumpet

Observe what vibrates when you blow into a horn. Make one in the Try This Activity.

TRY THIS **Activity!**

Make a Straw Horn!

What You Need

straw   scissors   ***Activity Log***

What To Do

1. Use your scissors to cut the end of the straw to make a shape like an arrow.
2. Flatten the straw by sliding your fingers up and down the length of it.
3. Now blow through the pointed end of the straw. Keep trying until you make a sound. What is vibrating? Write what you think in your ***Activity Log.***

What Happens to the Vibrations?

When one object begins to vibrate, things around it begin to vibrate, too. How do you think the vibrations move from one object to another? Do the next Try This Activity to find out.

TRY THIS Activity!

Watch the Waves!

What You Need

water
dish or pan
dropper
Activity Log

Put water in the dishpan so that it is half full. Fill the dropper with water. Make drops fall into the water in the pan, one at a time. Observe how the waves move. In your ***Activity Log,*** draw a picture of what you observe. What does this model show you about the way vibrations move?

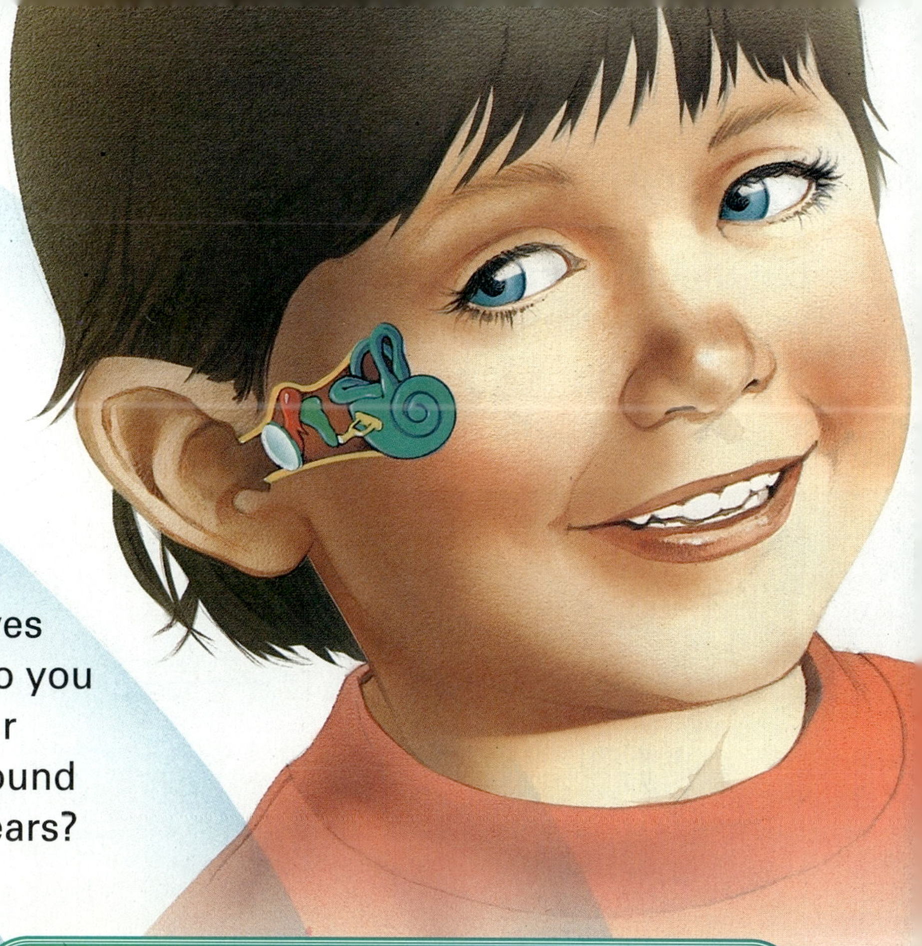

Sound vibrations move in waves. If you could see them, they would move like the waves in the dishpan. Do you know how we hear sound once the sound waves reach our ears?

This is how we hear sound.

- **Sound waves** move through the air until they reach the eardrum inside the ear.
- The vibrating sound waves cause the eardrum to vibrate, too.
- The vibrations move through the ear to nerves in the head.
- The nerves send messages to the brain. The brain tells us about the sounds we hear.

Underwater Sounds

Elena and Nico went swimming one day. Nico even made sounds under the water. Sound waves move through the air, but they also move through water. Dolphins and whales make sounds that move through water.

Dolphins make a lot of different whistling and clicking sounds. Dolphins call to each other. There are even sounds dolphins make to tell others when they are in trouble.

Humpback whales repeat sounds over and over, like a song. Scientists have taped sounds made by dolphins and whales.

Sound moves through air and water. Air is a gas and water is a liquid. Can sound move through something solid? Try it and find out.

TRY THIS **Activity!** ***String Talk!***

What You Need

paper cups
cotton string
paper clips
Activity Log
yarn
fishing line
sharpened pencil

What To Do

1. Use the pencil to poke a hole in the bottom of two cups.
2. Poke one end of a piece of yarn through the hole in the bottom of one cup. Tie the end of the yarn to the paper clip so that the paper clip is inside the cup. Tie the other end of the yarn inside the other cup.
3. Have a partner hold one cup. Pull the yarn tight between the two cups. Listen as your partner talks into the cup. Talk back while your partner listens.
4. Do steps 1, 2, and 3 again with other cups and the string. Repeat the activity again using fishing line. Write what happens each time in your ***Activity Log.***

Did sound move through all of the solids? Which solid made the best telephone? Why do you think so?

Moving Out—and Out and Out!

Even Nico's shoes are noisy! Elena heard him outside her room. SQUEAK! SQUEAK!

If sound waves are moving, where do they go? Doing the next activity should show you.

TRY THIS Activity!

Where Do Sound Waves Go?

What You Need

bell
Activity Log

What To Do

1. Ask a partner to stand and ring the bell. Stand in front of your partner and listen. Now stand behind your partner. Do you hear the sound?
2. Stand on one side of your partner. Do you hear the sound?
3. Walk to the back of the room and listen. Can you still hear the sound?
4. Walk outside the room and around the corner. Do you still hear the sound? What happens if you touch the bell when it is ringing? In your ***Activity Log,*** write about how the sound waves moved.

Sound waves move out in all directions. They keep moving until they hit something. If they hit a rug or curtains or furniture they are absorbed, the way water is absorbed by a sponge. The sound waves stop moving.

But if there is nothing to absorb the sound, the sound waves bounce off objects. They are reflected. Sound that is reflected can cause an **echo.** Have you ever heard your echo?

SCIENCE TECHNOLOGY AND Society Focus on Technology

Sound Engineers

Sound engineers help design many buildings. Some factories and schools are designed so that sound is absorbed. Why do you think that might be important? What kinds of materials might help make buildings quieter?

How Are Sounds Different?

Sometimes Nicholás is a one-man band! Think of some things that make sounds. How are the sounds different?

Minds On! What are some words that describe different sounds? Make a list in your ***Activity Log.***

EXPLORE

Activity!

Straw Symphony

You know we can make sounds by striking, plucking, strumming, or blowing into something. But how can we change a sound? How can we make different sounds?

What You Need

What To Do

1. Make one straw horn like the one you made in the activity on page 13.

2. Cut another straw in half and make a shorter horn. What kind of sound do you think it will make? Write what you predict in your ***Activity Log.***

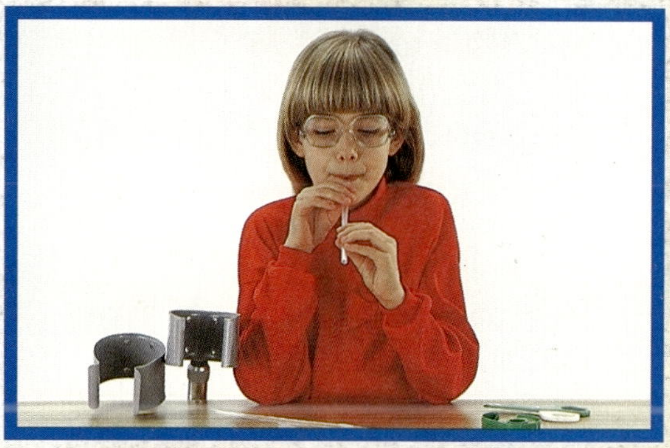

3. Tape two straws together and make a long horn. How do you think its sound will be different? Write what you predict in your ***Activity Log.***

4. Blow into each horn. Observe the different sounds. Write in your ***Activity Log*** about what you learned.

5. Use your pencil to poke a hole in the bottom of each cup. Put a cup on the end of each horn. Blow into the horns again, one at a time. Observe how the sounds change. Write about what you learned in your ***Activity Log.***

Safety! Be careful with the pencil when you poke the hole in your cup.

What Happened?

1. How were the sounds of the straw horns different?
2. What happened when you added the paper cups?
3. Why do you think musical instruments make different sounds?

High and Low

Elena takes piano lessons. Sometimes Nico pretends he knows how to play. One day he found the high notes at one end of the keyboard and the low notes at the other end. When the piano tuner came to tune the piano, Nico was curious. He looked inside the piano to see how it makes different sounds.

Little hammers inside the piano strike against strings. The strings are different lengths.

Low keys have long, thick strings. These strings vibrate slowly and make low sounds.

The highness or lowness of sound is called **pitch**. When something vibrates slowly, it has a lower pitch. When something vibrates quickly, it has a higher pitch.

High keys have short, thin strings. They vibrate quickly and make high sounds.

CAREERS The Piano Tuner

A piano tuner knows how to make sure each piano string has the right pitch. The tuner uses special tools to tighten loose strings.

A wedge keeps thick strings from vibrating while the tuner tightens other strings. Some keys have three strings. The tuner uses a damper to keep two strings from vibrating while tightening the third.

Minds On! Do you remember your shoe box "guitar"? Why do you think the rubber bands made different sounds?

You can experiment again with pitch. How can you make the sounds in the bottles higher or lower in this activity?

TRY THIS Activity! *Make a Bottle Organ!*

What You Need

6 clear, empty juice bottles
wooden spoon
water
Activity Log

What To Do

1. Pour a different amount of water into each bottle.
2. Carefully tap each bottle with the wooden spoon. What do you observe?
3. Put the bottles in order from the lowest to the highest sound. What do you observe about the levels of water?

What do you think vibrates to make the sounds? How could you change the sound in a bottle? Write what you think in your ***Activity Log.***

Follow That Note!

Use the bottle organ you made on page 26 and number the bottles from one to six. Play this song or sing this song with your friends. Which notes have a higher pitch? Which have a lower pitch?

Minds On! Put your hand on your throat and sing a high note. Now sing a low note. Two cords in your throat vibrate when you sing or talk. Muscles in your throat can make the cords shorter or longer. What do you think happens to the cords when you sing high? When you sing low?

Turn It Up! Turn It Down!

Nico's father says "turn it down" a lot. Can you guess why?

Minds On! Make soft sounds by whispering, tip-toeing, or patting your hands. Now make each of those sounds louder. What do you do to make each sound louder?

You can make a sound louder if you **amplify** it. A megaphone amplifies sound by sending all the sound waves in one direction.

Some amplifiers make sounds so loud they hurt your ears.

Remember that sound is a form of energy. The more energy you use to make a sound, the stronger the vibrations will be. The stronger the vibrations, the louder the sound. The loudness or softness of a sound is called its **volume.**

Minds On! Make Your Own Amplifiers! Turn on a radio or tape player or computer. Stand facing away from it and observe the sound. Cup your hands around your ears so that your hands face the sound. What difference do you observe? ●

Noise Annoys

"Nico, my boy,
noise annoys!"
said his father.

Some sounds are pleasant, but some are not. Unpleasant sounds are called **noise.** Look at the photograph. What sounds might be noise?

SCIENCE TECHNOLOGY AND Society

Focus on Environment

Dangerous Sounds

Noise can be so loud it is dangerous. It can harm people's hearing by hurting the nerves inside their ears. When people work at jobs where the noise is dangerously loud, laws say they must wear some kind of ear protection. When noise causes a problem, it is called noise pollution.

Some laws control noise pollution. The hours when jet planes can fly over homes are often controlled by law. What noises would you control if you could? How would you do it?

"We need ear protectors around this house!" said Elena. She was fed up with Nicholás. Mom took Nico out of the house for a whole day. Guess what? Elena missed him!

Glossary/Index

amplify, page 28
When you amplify a sound, you make it louder.

echo, page 20
An echo is made when sound bounces off an object such as a wall.

engineer, page 20
An engineer uses knowledge of the properties of matter and the sources of energy to design buildings, machines, or products.

noise, page 30
Noise is unpleasant sound.

noise pollution, page 31
When sounds are too annoying or harmful, they are called noise pollution.

pitch, page 25
The highness or lowness of a sound is called pitch.

sound waves, page 15
Sound waves can travel through solids, liquids, and gases.

vibrate, page 8
When strings vibrate, they move back and forth.

vibrations, page 9
Vibrations will make sound.

volume, page 29
The loudness or softness of a sound is called its volume.